Healing Through Expression
A Poetry Devotional Book

by Tiffany A. Selden

Poems, Reflections, and Affirmations for the Journey to Wholeness

For inquiries, collaborations, or speaking engagements:

tiffanyaselden@gmail.com

Cover and artwork by Cre Lily

Printed in the United States of America

Isn't She Grayt

PUBLISHING

All Scripture quotations in this devotional are taken from the **Easy-to-Read Version (ERV)** of the Bible.

DEDICATION

To My Beloved Husband, Patrick

You are my calm, my anchor, my safe place.

Thank you for loving me with such grace and patience.

You've given me room to heal, dream, and become.

I thank God for you every day.

I love you, always.

ACKNOWLEDGEMENTS

Christina, thank you for seeing me, speaking to me, and reminding me of what God had been trying to heal. Your words shifted something in me that I will never forget.

To my children, Aundrea, Imani, and Patrick Jr., thank you for loving me even when I was learning to love myself. We've grown up together in many ways, and I thank God for the grace, humor, and patience we've all needed to get here. You have challenged me and made me a better woman, not just a mother.

AUTHOR'S NOTE

I've always had this feeling deep down inside that my life was supposed to be used for something meaningful. I didn't always know what that meant, but the tug was real. Even when life was life-ing and I was just trying to stay afloat, a part of me always believed that what I survived would eventually help somebody else.

Now, let's be very clear. I used to think my purpose would show up through singing. I really did. In my head, I was going to minister to the masses in song like one of my favorite gospel artist CeCe Winans. The only problem was that God did not bless me with the gift of singing. At all. But does that stop me from having my CeCe playlist blasting while I'm in the kitchen or the car, singing loud and wrong. Absolutely not. God accepts all worship. Even the off-key kind.

And let me tell you how funny God is. I couldn't sing… yet somehow my poems became inspiration for a song. A whole song. A real melody, a real track *(All the Things I Ever Wanted to Do), like it was gently tapping me on the shoulder saying, "See! You may not be CeCe, but you still got something to say." That moment reminded me healing shows up, however it wants to sometimes as a poem, sometimes as a song, sometimes in a way you never expected.

Since singing wasn't my lane, I leaned into the part of me that has always been creative. I started doing abstract art just for fun. I never called myself an artist until people started buying my work. One piece turned into another, then another, then a few more. Before I knew it, I found myself whispering, now wait a minute… I think I might actually be an artist. That's how my work as Cre Lily began.

And honestly, the same thing happened with writing. I didn't sit down planning to write a poetry devotional book. Words just started coming out of me after an encounter that shook something loose in my spirit. A

Nurse Practitioner named Christina said things to me that I know only God could have shown her. She spoke to places I had tucked away for years and made it clear that it was time for me to start healing the parts of myself I had been avoiding. That moment changed my life, and it opened the door to this book.

I'm not a theologian. I'm not a scholar. I'm not someone with all the answers. I'm simply a woman who has lived, grown, messed up, healed, and learned how to be honest with herself. These poems came from the same place my healing came from: prayer, quiet moments, and a desire to finally walk in who God created me to be.

I've written journals and I'll probably write a few more books before I leave this world. But this one right here is different. This one came from the deepest part of me. The part that finally stopped hiding. The part that finally exhaled.

My hope is that as you read, something opens in you too. Something softens. Something lets go. And maybe, just maybe, you find a piece of yourself in these pages.

Thank you for being here,

Tiffany

PREFACE

Healing Through Expression: A Poetry Devotional Book

There are moments in life when you think you're just living your routine, and then God steps in and says, "No, daughter, I have something else for you." This book was born out of one of those moments. I wasn't journaling. I wasn't doing deep emotional work.
I wasn't sitting in prayer or meditation.

I was in urgent care again.

Same stomach pain I'd been dealing with for years. Same building. Same routine. I had been there so often that when the radiology tech came to get me for my CT scan, she looked at the chart and said, "Oh yes, we know Mrs. Selden well." At that point, I didn't know if I needed healing or an employee badge.

But something was different that day.

The Nurse Practitioner who walked in was someone I had never seen before. A Black woman like me, with a calm and steady presence that made the room feel different the moment she entered. Her mask covered most of her face, but her eyes were warm and focused, almost like she was paying attention to more than just symptoms. Her name was Christina.

She asked me the usual questions, also what surprised me she asked, "Are you a Christian?" She stepped out, and the tech took me to get the CT scan. When Christina returned afterward, she sat down with intention, the kind of posture people use when they're not just there to talk about test results. She asked if she could speak to me woman to woman and believer to believer. I told her yes.

That's when everything shifted.

She told me she felt led by God to share some things with me. That the pain I was experiencing might be tied to childhood trauma I had spent years trying not to face. Then she asked me gently, "Did you have a traumatic childhood?"

I didn't even answer. The tears answered for me.

She told me it was time for me to start facing what had been buried so I could finally walk in my true purpose. And I remember thinking, "Lord… I've been married over thirty-six years, raised three children, have two grandchildren, worked, lived, pushed through life, and you're telling me I haven't even stepped into my purpose yet?" But deep down, I knew what she meant. I had been surviving, not healing.

Then she said something I never expected to hear in an exam room.

She told me she could feel the presence of my grandmother and my ancestors around me, and that my grandmother was right there with me. She said it with such gentleness and sincerity that something inside me reacted at once. Not fear. Not confusion. Just a deep awareness that touched a place I had been carrying quietly for years.

My grandmother and I had a complicated relationship. I didn't even attend her funeral. I had held on to guilt I never talked about. And Christina, who knew nothing about me or my past, began speaking into those very places. She spoke about my grandmother with warmth and compassion. Nothing dark or dramatic. Nothing disrespectful to God. Just the kind of spiritual moment that brings truth to the surface.

Then she said words my mother had told me my grandmother spoke before she passed. Hearing them again, from someone who had no way of knowing, felt like God making sure I didn't miss the message.

When the appointment was over, I asked the nurse if I could speak to Christina again, and she told me Christina wasn't available. And in my spirit, I knew that moment wasn't meant to be repeated. It was something God allowed just once, exactly when I needed it.

I walked out of that building feeling lighter. I suddenly didn't understand everything, but something inside me had opened. Guilt began to lift. Memories settled differently. And for the first time in a long time, I felt a quiet release.

Later that night, I sat down with my laptop. No outline. No big plan. Just honesty pouring out. The words came gently and freely, almost like breathing.

That moment became the beginning of this book.

Every poem, every reflection, every affirmation in these pages grew out of that place where truth finally met peace and where God met me exactly where I was.

My hope is that something in these pages meets you too.

INTRODUCTION

Bridge to Healing: A Journey from Brokenness to Becoming Whole

I didn't write this book because I have all the answers.
I wrote it because, for a long time, I didn't even know where to begin.

There were seasons in my life when I felt disconnected from myself, like I was moving through the world carrying pieces of a story I didn't know how to name yet. I was trying to be strong, trying to push through, trying to pretend things didn't hurt as deeply as they did. But God has a way of meeting you right where you are, even when you don't recognize the moment as holy.

Healing, for me, wasn't one big breakthrough. It was a series of quiet moments, small, almost unnoticeable shifts that slowly pulled me back into myself. A conversation I didn't expect. A reflection I wasn't ready for. A prayer whispered at the right time. A reminder that I was created with purpose, even in the seasons when I felt lost.

These poems came out of those moments.
They're not polished ideas or church-girl clichés.
They're my real-life conversations with God, my own heart, and the woman I was becoming. I didn't write them to sound perfect. I wrote them to sound true.

And somewhere along the way, I realized something important: healing isn't something you arrive at, it's something you grow into. It's a process. A journey. A daily "yes" to becoming whole. This book is the bridge I built between who I used to be and who I'm becoming. My prayer is that, as you walk across it, something in your own journey becomes clearer, that you feel less alone, more seen, and more connected to the version of you God has been patiently calling forward. You don't have to rush. You don't have to have it all figured out. You don't have to pretend you're fine. Just walk with me, page by page. Let the poems speak to you. Let the reflections settle in your spirit. Let the affirmations remind you of what's still possible. This isn't just a devotional. It's a gentle invitation. A soft place to land.

A reminder that becoming whole is not about doing more it's about finally coming home to yourself.

Welcome to your own journey of awakening, healing, becoming, and rising.

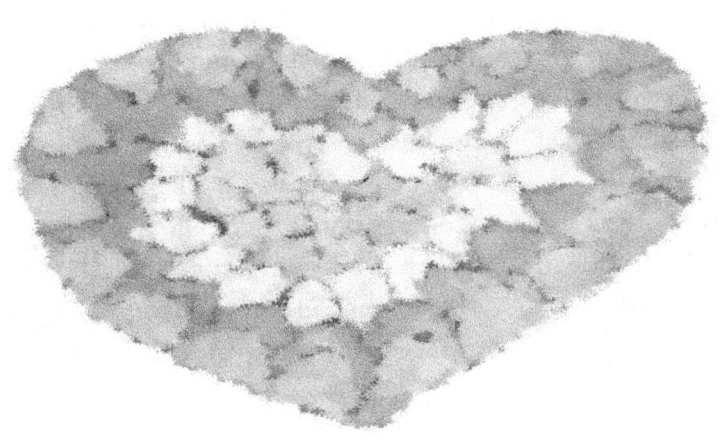

CHAPTER ONE - AWAKENING

Get up and shine, for your light has come and the glory of the Lord rises upon you.
Isaiah 60:1

Awakening feels like that moment when your soul finally exhales. Not because everything in your life suddenly makes sense, but because something inside you has shifted. It's the quiet turning point when you stop running from yourself and start letting God show you who you've always been beneath the fear, the hurt, and the stories life tried to write for you. It doesn't shout. It shows up gently, almost like a soft reminder of the you that existed before the trauma, before the doubt, before life tried to shrink your identity. Even in the seasons when you felt stuck or surrounded by darkness, God was moving in ways you didn't see yet. And then a little light breaks through. Maybe not enough to understand everything, but enough to take one step. Awakening isn't about becoming someone new. It's remembering yourself. The real you. The one God intended. And when God calls you forward, something in your spirit recognizes it's time. Not because you suddenly feel brave, but because you know you can't go back to who you were before.

AS OF TODAY, I AM FREE

As of today, I no longer walk in the ideas or opinions of others
nor in the weight of caring what they think of me.
I set myself free.

I am wondrously made,
a daughter of God,
poured full of His grace,
free to explore all He has placed before me.

I live in abundance,
fully aware that loving me
is the truest way of being me.

I take back my dignity
not in superiority,
but in divine authority.
I claim my dignity.

I release those who cannot love me well,
and I bless them as they go.
I make room for those who know how to love me
with authenticity, empathy, and compassion.

I am free from the wounded child
who once lived inside me,
for I have turned that pain over,
and I am free.

My Father gave His life
so that I could live free,
free to walk in peace,
even amid life's complexities.

As of today,
I am free.

- ♥ **Reflection:** Sometimes awakening begins with choosing yourself again, even if it's for the first time.
- ♥ **Affirmation:** I honor the freedom God is growing in me.

THE MIRROR

One day I walked past the mirror,
at thirty years old to be exact.
I had to double back,
and what did I see?

More than a reflection.
I saw the woman God had been shaping me to be.

There were lessons, heartbreaks,
and countless prayers through the years.
My eyes told stories of endurance,
no longer shadowed by darkness,
despair, restlessness, or lack of hope.

They reflected a heart that carried wounds,
now covered in wisdom,
the first glimpse of beauty that lay within.

For years, I didn't know
the beauty I carried, inside or out.

I didn't flinch at my own reflection.
I simply stood there, still,
wondering how I had spent so long
not knowing it was always there.

I didn't flinch at my own beauty,
nor did I despair
at the thought of never seeing it before.

I smiled,
not because I am flawless,
but because I am free.

The voices of my past
have finally lost their hold on me.

And as I stood before that mirror,
it didn't judge me,
it honored me.

It reminded me
that healing looks good on me.

- ♥ **Reflection:** Sometimes awakening shows up in your own reflection when you finally recognize the woman you've grown into.
- ♥ **Affirmation:** I honor the woman I am becoming.

BE STILL, MY SOUL

Be still, my soul.
You have run long enough.

You have spent too many years
trying to prove you are enough
to people who could not see your worth.

Lay it down
the heavy burden,
the endless striving,
the need to be understood.

A whisper rose in my spirit:
You were never meant to earn love.
You were born from it.

Be still,
for the One who made you
dwells within you.

Let peace find you.

For in the stillness,
you will see,
you will remember,
you will return
to who you truly are
and to whom you belong.

💜 **Reflection:** Stillness has a gentle way of reminding you that peace was always waiting for you.

♥ **Affirmation:** I allow myself to rest and trust what God is doing in me.

♥ Closing Reflection

Awakening isn't a destination. It's simply the moment you tell the truth to yourself and let God meet you there. As you keep turning these pages, give yourself permission to grow at your own pace. You don't have to rush your healing. Just stay open.

CHAPTER TWO – HEALING

He heals their broken hearts and bandages their wounds.
Psalm 147:3

Healing isn't loud or dramatic. It comes in those quiet moments when you stop telling yourself you're fine and finally let your heart breathe. It shows up when you stop carrying everything alone, when you stop pushing down the pain, when you let yourself feel what's been waiting to be understood.

Healing has never been about erasing the past. It's been about learning how to sit with it without falling apart, about letting God touch the places you've tried to ignore, about allowing the old memories to loosen their grip. It's noticing how something that once felt like it owned you now passes through you more gently.

This season of healing softens everything the heart, the memories, the tone of your inner voice. You speak to yourself differently. You choose yourself differently. You don't rush your way through things anymore because you know healing isn't a sprint, it's slow unfolding.

And the beautiful thing about healing is that it meets you exactly where you are. It doesn't demand perfection. It doesn't ask you to hurry. It walks beside you at the pace your spirit can handle, one tender step at a time.

Little by little, you realize the pain doesn't hit as hard. You stop bracing for what hurts you before. You trust more, breathe deeper, and feel safer in your own skin. That's healing the quiet return of strength, peace, and the parts of you that were waiting to come back home.

WOUNDED CHILD

I used to carry her with me everywhere,
like a badge of honor, living in despair.

The little girl inside me,
afraid of being unseen,
afraid of not being enough.

Constant feelings of rejection.
Feeling disapproved of.
Shrinking myself to fit in,
always afraid of being accused of being too much.

I ached for acceptance everywhere I went.
I loved hard and people-pleased harder,
and still found dead ends.
Relationships slipped away
because even betraying myself to keep them
was never enough.

One day, I met her with open arms.
I told her she was safe.
I told her God never left her.

The rejection she felt
was really His blessing and protection,
proof she never needed to force herself to fit anywhere.

I watched as peace replaced her trembling.
Where fear once lived,
joy returned to her eyes.

Never shrink.
Never turn away.

God walks beside her
every step of the way.

Together, we are whole
the woman I've become
and the child I have forgiven.

- ♥ **Reflection:** Sometimes healing starts when you finally turn toward the parts of you that were hurting and tell them they're safe now.
- ♥ **Affirmation:** I offer compassion to every version of me.

GRACE IN THE GARDEN

There were places I thought I'd never smile again,
even as I walked through my own garden.
Memories of trauma fluttered in like restless winds,
but my Creator, in tender mercy,
walked me through the weeds of my pain
and showed me beauty I had missed again and again.

I began to see strength where there was once sorrow,
hope rising for a brighter tomorrow.
I realized the weeds were not my ending.
They were wrapped around branches for my growth,
the roots of my new beginning.

Grace blooms there still,
The soft and steady as the soil is tilled,
reminding me that even broken ground,
when tended with care,
can grow gardens of peace abound.

- ❤ **Reflection:** Healing often shows up like a slow bloom small, steady, and full of grace even in places you thought nothing good could grow.
- ❤ **Affirmation:** I welcome the gentle ways the Creator is renewing me.

♥ Closing Reflection

Healing isn't always pretty, but it is always sacred. Every time you choose honesty over avoidance, or gentleness over judgment, something softens inside you. Let this chapter remind you that you're not behind. You're becoming whole in ways you can't always see yet.

CHAPTER THREE - BECOMING

Anyone who belongs to Christ has become a new person. The old life is gone; a new life has begun.
2 Corinthians 5:17

Becoming isn't a sudden transformation. It doesn't show up with fireworks or applause. It's quieter than that almost subtle the slow unfolding of the woman God always knew you would be.

It happens in the moments after healing begins to settle in your bones.
When you start standing a little taller without even noticing.
When your "no" gets clearer, your "yes" gets softer, and your peace becomes something you protect without guilt.

Becoming is that gentle but steady shift where you stop abandoning yourself.
Where you stop performing strength and actually feel it.
Where you stop apologizing for taking up space you were created to fill.

This part of the journey feels different because you feel different.
You're not trying to prove anything anymore.
You're simply aligning with who God says you are and letting that be enough.

Becoming isn't about perfection.
It's about acceptance, honesty, and courage.
It's about walking like a woman who knows she belongs to God fully, securely, and without question.

And the beautiful thing is... you don't have to rush this part.
You grow into it. You rise into it.
You become into it day by day, layer by layer, grace by grace.

This is the chapter where you meet the version of yourself you prayed for.
And she is ready.

WONDROUSLY MADE

There is a divine fingerprint on my soul,
etched by the hands of a loving Creator
determined to make me whole.

No flaw can erase it,
no failure can diminish it.

I am made of His light.
He breathes life into me
a God-given sacred design
that shaped and named me.

When I doubt myself,
I return to the truth:

I am not random.
I am not mistaken.
I am not a failure.
I am not just anybody.

I am chosen.
I am known.
I am wondrously made.

- ♥ **Reflection:** Becoming often starts with remembering who you already are. Sometimes the real growth is learning to see yourself the way God has seen you the whole time.
- ♥ **Affirmation:** I embrace the truth that I am made with intention and purpose.

CALLING BACK MY SOVEREIGNTY

There was a time I gave away my peace.
To please others with fear of them leaving me.

I handed over my voice,
my time,
my worth,
my peace piece by piece,
only for them not to appreciate me.

God whispered and said, "Daughter, that's enough.
It's time you return home to yourself."

So, I did.

I called back my spirit
from every person, place, and thing.
I gathered my strength
to love me right again.

My softness,
my laughter,
my light
I wrapped them around me
like a prayer shawl
and stood tall.

This was not pride.
It was a remembrance of me.

I am not above anyone,
but I walk now in the authority
of who He says I am.

Not afraid of being alone,
I call back my sovereignty.

I am whole.
I am healed.
I am free
walking fully
in God's authority.

- ♥ **Reflection:** There comes a moment when you realize how much of yourself you gave away and decide to bring every piece back home. That decision alone is growth.
- ♥ **Affirmation:** I reclaim the parts of me I lost along the way.

THE RHYTHM OF BECOMING

I used to wonder if I would ever be healed,
measuring my progress
like a cup of detergent
poured into a washer,
waiting to be filled.

But God reminded me:
just as you place the laundry in the washer,
pour that detergent,
and wait for the water to rise,
in you, I am alive.

I have washed you in My blood,
and filled you with My Spirit,
watching from above.

He whispered,
"Trust the rhythm of My timing,
like the hum of the washer's drum,
and what you are becoming."

Some days, I am the detergent,
cleansing what clings too tightly.

Some days, I am the washer,
holding what needs to be renewed.

Some days, I am the drum,
turning in rhythm with grace.

But all days,
I am growing, unfolding,

and washed in His blood
and that is enough.

- ♥ **Reflection:** Becoming has its own rhythm. Some days you're pouring into yourself, and other days you're simply letting God hold you. Both matters. Both counts.
- ♥ **Affirmation:** I trust the timing of who I am becoming.

♥ Closing Reflection

Becoming is really just remembering who you were before life tried to change your story. You're not trying to "fix" yourself, you're learning to honor the person God designed you to be. Give yourself credit for the ways you've grown, even the quiet changes no one else sees.

CHAPTER FOUR - NO LONGER SHRINKING

Where the Spirit of the Lord is, there is freedom.
2 Corinthians 3:17

There comes a moment in your journey when you quietly decide, I'm not shrinking anymore.
Not out of anger.
Not out of pride.
But because your spirit finally understands it was never meant to live small.

This part of becoming isn't loud it's a calm, steady confidence that rises after years of second-guessing, overthinking, and trying to fit into places that were never meant to hold you. You start noticing the ways you used to fold yourself down just to make others comfortable, and something in you says, No more.

It's not about proving anything.
It's not about showing anyone you've changed.
It's about honoring the woman God has shaped you into the woman who has survived, learned, healed, and grown.

No longer shrinking feels like breathing deeper.
It feels like choosing peace without apologizing for it.
It feels like walking into a room without dimming your light to match someone else's insecurity.
It feels like knowing your worth without needing validation to confirm it.

This chapter marks the shift from internal healing to external confidence.
It's where your boundaries strengthen.
Your voice steadies.
Your presence settles.

And your heart stops negotiating with things that were never aligned with you in the first place.

You don't have to be loud about it.
You just choose not to shrink.
And that choice changes everything.

GARBAGE HAS A WAY OF TAKING ITSELF OUT

I have a saying I live by now:
the garbage has a way of taking itself out.

I learned long ago when people get loud,
there's no need to scream or shout.
Just sit back, breathe, and let it be.
Don't waste your peace or your energy.

What's meant to stay will always stay,
and what's not meant will drift away.

Life reveals the truth in time
no need to force, defend, or climb.

Those who walk in light will stand;
those who don't will fade like sand.

So I keep my spirit calm and clean,
unbothered, steady, and serene.

If it leaves, it served its role;
if it stays, it feeds my soul.

Let love be my filter,
and silence my grace.

The garbage takes itself out,
and peace returns to fill that space.

- ♥ **Reflection:** Sometimes the biggest shift comes when you stop fighting for what was never meant to stay.
- ♥ **Affirmation:** I protect my peace without apology.

WHEW, CHILE! I WAS A MESS!

No matter what I did, my mind could never find rest.

I worried, overthought, and tried to make sense

of things God never asked me to fix.

It wasn't until I learned to sit still,
to breathe, to meditate, and to pray,
that He began to lift the weight
of overthinking away.

In the stillness, I began to see
He was aligning His Word and His will within me.

Each quiet moment, each prayer-filled day,
writing these poems became my healing,
my sacred way.

Now I stand renewed and free,
grateful for what this journey
has done in me.

And it is my prayer, as you read these words today,
that they bring you peace
and make you whole
in that same holy way.

- ♥ **Reflection:** Growth gets real when you can look back on your chaos and laugh a little.
- ♥ **Affirmation:** I welcome clarity, confidence, and peace.

THE COURAGE TO BE ME

I spent years trying to fit into boxes
afraid to be me.
Into boxes I was never meant to see.

I held back from speaking
when my spirit wanted to roar.
Hid my awareness, instincts, and intuition
so others wouldn't see
that I already knew their ill intentions,
because that knowing lived deep within me.

I hid my disappointment, never letting on
that their spirit was unsettling
and I wanted them gone.

But courage is a quiet awakening
that rises from within.
It began as a whisper,
telling me to leave them alone
and let them be.

I stepped into the light
with no time to spare.
I let them go
and my purpose became clear.

I began to see myself
without shedding a tear.

I am not arrogant.
I am not rebellious.

I am obedient
to the truth of who God created me to be.

I no longer shrink for comfort
nor ignore what I feel.
I live in an abundance
of peace and joy.

I walk forward with open hands,
knowing that courage is not the absence of fear.
It is seeing who I am with God
loud and clear.

- ♥ **Reflection:** Courage grows in quiet moments right when you finally stop dimming your own light.
- ♥ **Affirmation:** I show up as my full self with peace and confidence.

NOT THAT DEEP

I've been in moments where people have said,
"You're not that deep,"
pretending those words weren't meant for me.
And I always think,
that's something I never claimed to be.
I'm just being me.

If that's so, then why come to me?
I never exalted myself,
never acted like I could part a sea.
I simply live in the space
where I believe God appointed me to be,
guided by His presence,
led by His Word.

Do not think yourself higher,
because truth be told,
we are not above anyone,
and not below.
We are made in the image of the Creator,
His children, because He told us so.

I've learned to walk through this life
confident and bold,
but not without trials,
not without reflection,
not without learning what His Word can mold.

So I write this not to throw shade,
but as a gentle reminder,
a cautionary tale:

If you use your words to dim someone's light
in the spirit of meanness,
especially a child of God,
you will fail.

Because when you do the work,
you learn to walk healed and whole,
fully aware of who you are becoming.
And in that becoming,
you break the mold.

- ♥ **Reflection:** Not everyone will understand your depth and that's perfectly fine.
- ♥ **Affirmation:** I stay true to who I am, no explanations needed.

REMEMBER MY NAME

They looked at me and laughed,
and trust me, I was fully aware.
But I couldn't help but wonder,
did you really think I'd care?

I don't step into your space;
you choose to come into mine.
If my light draws your attention,
that's between you and the Divine.

You laugh as if you hold something over me,
but truth be told,
I stand as I do
because the love of my Father in Heaven
has taught me to be bold.

So while you're laughing,
don't expect me to shrink,
to curl up, to fold, or retreat.
I was never built to crumble
only to rise, to reflect, to repeat.

And because you tried to break me,
I learned to bend instead.
You thought you planted doubt,
but you watered strength instead.

So thank you for the lesson,
for the mirror, for the motivation.
Every test became transformation;
every sting, a spark of liberation.

I walk lighter now, free and clear,
no bitterness, no need to blame.
Just gratitude for the growth
and the courage to stand in my name.

- 💜 **Reflection:** Sometimes the very things meant to break you end up revealing your strength.
- 💜 **Affirmation:** I stand tall in the woman God designed me to be.

♥ Closing Reflection

No longer shrinking means you've stopped handing your power away. There is a strength that rises when you finally stop dimming your light. Let this chapter be your reminder that confidence isn't arrogance, it's clarity. You deserve to take up space in every room God sends you into.

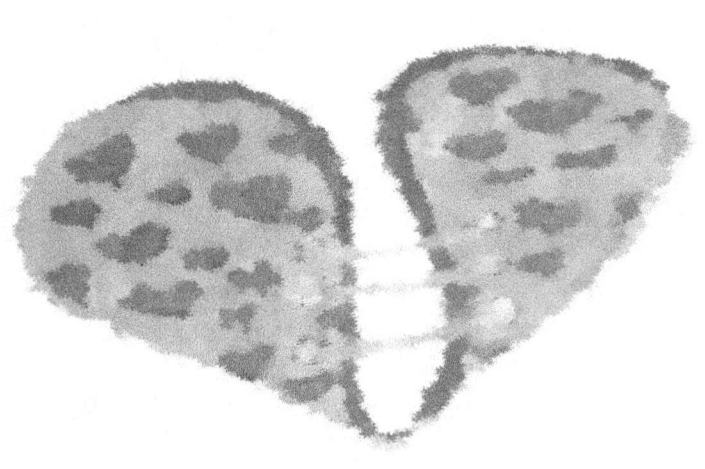

CHAPTER FIVE - LOVE

God is love, and when we choose love, we choose Him.
1 John 4:16

Love, for me, shifted when I finally learned to let it meet me where I am instead of where I used to be. I used to chase love, question it, overthink it, or brace myself for it to disappear. Now I understand that real love doesn't run. It doesn't rush. It doesn't demand that you perform to be worth it.

Real love feels like breath after holding it too long.

It shows up patiently. It grows slowly. And it teaches you how to open your heart without losing yourself in the process.

I had to unlearn a lot to get here. Love used to feel like proving I was worthy of it or working overtime to be chosen. But God's love has a way of settling you. It makes you softer without making you weak. It makes you open without making you naive. It teaches you that love isn't something you chase; it's something you allow.

This chapter is about that shift.
The shift into love that stays.
Love that heals.
Love that doesn't drain you or shrink you.
Love that feels grown, steady, and safe.

May these poems remind you of what love looks like when God is in it.

SET FREE BY LOVE

Love didn't find me
it was always there.
It surrounded me
in everything I held dear.

The sunrise is steady and warm,
drawing me near,
wanting to know more.

Love didn't demand that I change.
It reminded me I was like the sun
I had the light in me;
I was already enough.

"Rise, you are safe,
you are Mine.
Remember My Son.
He died so you could walk,
get up,
and run."

And in that whisper,
the walls that blocked the sunlight
and the Son
fell away,
and I realized
I was never meant to fight for love
it was there all along.

I was made from it.
Set free with it.
Kept by it.

Thanks to the sacrifice
of the Son.

- ♥ **Reflection:** Sometimes the real turning point is when you stop trying to earn love and let yourself receive the love that has been there all along.
- ♥ **Affirmation:** I don't have to fight for love. I am already loved by God.

OVERFLOW

I am no longer in search
of others to complete me.
My wholeness was never lost,
only forgotten,
covered beneath
the weight of pain.

Then God reminded me:
You were never broken
or beyond repair.
I was always there.

He said,
"Get up.
Gather the fragments
of your heart,
place them in My hands,
and never again
let us be apart."

He returned my heart to me
stronger, healed,
and beautifully whole.
Now when I love,
it doesn't take a toll.
I love from overflow,
with more room to grow.

I picked up my whole heart
with newfound courage in tow
healthier, stronger,
confident, and bold,

vowing never again
to sink so low.

Never again will I forget
the love of God
that lives inside me,
the love that never stands still
it flows.

- ♥ **Reflection:** Healing lets you love from a full place, not an empty one. You're allowed to let God restore you before you pour into anyone else.
- ♥ **Affirmation:** I love from overflow, not from empty places.

REFLECTION OF LOVE

When I love myself with tender care,
I honor the One who made me.

Every act of kindness toward my own heart
is His compassion reflected in me.

Every word of affirmation
is a quiet whisper of His love,
a prayer in motion,
a soft worship rising in my soul.

For I am not just His creation.
I am God's reflection of love.

So I speak to myself with patience,
with forgiveness,
with kindness,
with a love that does not run out.

- ♥ **Reflection:** The way you speak to yourself is part of your worship. You are allowed to talk to yourself like someone God deeply loves.
- ♥ **Affirmation:** I choose words that honor the woman God made me to be

LOVE THAT STAYS

The world teaches love that leaves.
But God teaches love that stays.

It stays when I stumble.
It stays when I question His love.
It stays when I forget my own worth.

It stands in the gap,
covers the places I outgrew,
and comforts the parts
I am still learning to live with.

Love that stays does not rush.
It doesn't shout.
It doesn't demand.

It holds.
It listens.
It forgives.

It brings peace into the room
before I even know I need it.
It reminds me gently
that nothing about me
is too much for God.

This is the love
that anchors my becoming
steady, patient, everlasting.
Not earned.
Not threatened.
Not fragile.

His love within me,
quiet and powerful,
teaching me how to stay
with myself too.

- ♥ **Reflection:** There is a difference between love that drains you and love that stands with you. You are worthy of the kind that stays and shows up.
- ♥ **Affirmation:** I am worthy of steady, faithful love.

A Love That God Gifted Me

I didn't have a rescuer.
I had a friend.

He saw something in me that most never did
light, a quiet strength,
a potential unseen even by my own kin.

He knew my fears,
and at times wiped my tears.
He stood by me steadfast and true,
and I thank the Lord above for that kind of love.

Not out of pity, this much I know
for I was there for him too,
through every high
and every low.

We would talk for hours,
sharing our hopes and dreams.
Never did I imagine his future plans
would one day include me.

I remember praying softly,
"God, if the things he wants are from You,
let them be."

Unbeknownst to me,
that prayer included me.

When he revealed his heart and asked,
"Will you marry me?"
I could barely speak.
"How could it be? Why would you choose me?"

You see, I was broken,
covered in shame.
My life choices had left their stain.

But he looked into my eyes and said,
"I've stood by you through it all.
Never once did I want you to fall.
Not from pity, no, that is true.
From the first day I met you,
you were honest, pure, and true.

When I had nothing, you stood near.
When I was lost, your friendship was clear.
I saw in you what others could not see
a heart that loves deeply, unconditionally.

So I prayed to God above,
'Am I right in wanting Tiffany as my wife?'
And He said, 'Yes, because her heart is true.
When you had nothing, she still chose you.'"

And so we began our journey
side by side.
It wasn't always easy,
but through every storm and every tide,
one thing remained constant and true:

my heart, once broken,
was healed by the love
of both God
and you.

- ♥ **Reflection:** Healthy love doesn't erase your past; it walks with you as you heal. You are not too broken to be chosen with care and intention.
- ♥ **Affirmation:** I am open to love that is patient, safe, and kind to my soul.

♥ Closing Reflection

Love, at its best, doesn't demand you become someone else. It teaches you how to soften, how to receive, and how to give without losing yourself. Whether it's God's love, your own love, or the love you share with others, let it lift you instead of weigh you down.

CHAPTER SIX - WHOLENESS

My grace is all you need. My power is strongest when you are weak.
2 Corinthians 12:9

Wholeness feels like finally being able to rest inside your own life. Not because everything is perfect, but because you're no longer breaking yourself to hold it all together. It's that quiet shift when your spirit stops bracing for what might go wrong and starts leaning into what God is making right.

It doesn't arrive loud or dramatic. It comes softly, almost like a gentle settling in your chest, a reminder that peace was never out of reach, only waiting for you to slow down long enough to feel it. Wholeness grows in the moments when you trust God enough to release the old stories, the old hurts, the old habits of shrinking or surviving.

There were seasons when you carried more than you ever spoke about. Times when you smiled your way through storms, stood up when you were exhausted, and loved others from an empty place. But even then, God was stitching you back together, piece by piece, teaching your heart a new rhythm.

And then one day, something shifts. You wake up and realize you're not fighting the same battles anymore. You're kinder to yourself. Your boundaries are stronger. Your thoughts are quieter. Your heart beats steadier.

Wholeness isn't about becoming a different version of yourself.
It's about returning to the version God always intended, the one who trusts, breathes, chooses peace, and stands whole from the inside out.

And when God invites you into that kind of peace, something in you finally agrees I don't have to live fractured anymore.

ANOINTED IN HONEY

I dreamed I was poured with honey
not the kind money could buy,
but the kind poured straight from heaven,
thick with grace and light.

It flowed over me slowly,
covering every wound that once cried out,
soothing every scar that told
the stories my soul tried to hide.

I stood there still, unafraid
feeling its warmth become my peace.

Then came a hum, soft at first:
a swarm of honeybees encircling me.
They did not sting; they sang.

Their buzzing was a hymn of healing,
a song of sweetness and renewal,
whispering, "You are whole again."

So I sat down, dipped my finger in a cup of tea
a taste of new spirit, a sip of serenity.

I leaned back, smiled, and said with ease,
"Alright, Honey it's good to be me."

♥ **Reflection:** Wholeness does not always arrive loud. Sometimes it feels like a slow sweetness returning to places that once felt numb. You are allowed to let life feel softer now, even if you are still getting used to that.

♥ **Affirmation:** I welcome sweetness, peace, and ease back into my life.

The Refuge of Stillness That Made Me Whole

Throughout the years, I feared almost everything,
everyone, even myself.
Surrounded by people, still felt alone.

But in the stillness, I found God waiting
not to fix me,
but to remind me
I was never alone.

He whispered, "You have nothing to fear,
for your Father still sits on the throne."

It was then that stillness became my refuge
a sacred place to bow my head and pray,
a sanctuary of praise,
where I could listen to my Father
and let Him lead the way.

No longer bound by fear,
I found strength in His presence each day.

At His feet, He planted me
rooted in peace,
grounded in love.

And there,
in the stillness,
I was never lonely again.
I was made whole.

♥ **Reflection:** Wholeness often grows in the quiet. When you give
yourself permission to slow down, breathe, and sit with God, you

start to feel held in a way people could never offer. Stillness becomes less scary and more like home.

- ♥ **Affirmation:** I let stillness be a safe place for me, and I trust God to meet me there.

GROW AND BLOOM

Some seasons felt too heavy to bear.
Rain poured longer with nothing to spare.
My heart ached waiting for my God to take me there
to my healing, to my growth, to my blooming.

When it happened, my eyes filled with tears.
I was overwhelmed by a world that was unkind.
But because God whispered to me, I began to understand
I'm here to take that away.

Grow where you are, bloom anyway.

Even when others doubted me,
even when life felt unfair,
I knew I was growing, I was blooming,
turning toward the light.

Rooted in the soil of my faith
deeper than any pain.

Now my roots are firmly planted,
every petal of my life sings:
You can heal,
you can grow,
you can bloom
again and again.

- ♥ **Reflection:** Growth doesn't always feel pretty when you're in it. But looking back, you'll see how every hard season helped you bloom in ways you didn't expect.
- ♥ **Affirmation:** I allow myself to grow at my own pace, in my own way.

♥ Closing Reflection

Wholeness isn't perfection. It's peace, a steady calm that reminds you you're no longer living in pieces. You're allowed to rest. You're allowed to breathe. And you're allowed to enjoy the version of yourself that fought so hard to get here.

CHAPTER SEVEN: LEGACY

One generation will praise Your works to another; they will declare Your mighty acts.
Psalm 145:4

Legacy, to me, isn't about things or accomplishments. It's not the titles we held or the way people described us in passing. Legacy is softer than that, more honest than that. It's the imprint your life leaves on hearts long after the moment has moved on.

It shows up in the way you learned to love after learning what love is not.
It shows up in the way you broke patterns that tried to follow you.
It shows up in the peace you fought for so your children and grandchildren wouldn't have to fight the same battles.

Legacy is not perfection. It's transformation.

It's choosing to heal so the next generation has a safer place to land.
It's standing firm in your truth, so your descendants don't inherit your silence.
It's becoming a woman who lives with intention, wisdom, and grace not just for yourself, but for everyone who comes after you.

At this point in my life, I see legacy as the quiet strength a woman carries after she's lived, learned, forgiven, and grown. It's the faith that held her together. The tenderness that surprised her. The courage that stayed with her when nothing else felt steady.

If I leave anything behind, I pray it's this:
that healing is real,
that God is faithful,
and that you are stronger than anything that ever tried to break you.

Legacy isn't just what you leave behind.

Legacy is who you become and the light that becomes possible because of it.

THE LIGHT THAT FOLLOWS ME

My words are breathed through quiet prayer,
Each one a seed of love and care.
Every line holds a piece of me,
Lessons shaped by grace's sea.

You are the light that follows near,
The echo of prayers God chose to hear.
I pray you live with truth untold,
And let your heart be pure and bold.

Speak in love through all you do,
Let peace within keep guiding you.
Perfection fades, just let it be,
For God made you perfectly.
So walk in faith, stand firm, be kind,
Keep heaven's promise in your mind.
You are my answered prayer, my song.
The light that leads my soul along.

♥ **Reflection:**
Love leaves a light behind it. When you speak with honesty and live with gentleness, your presence becomes a prayer that lingers long after the words are gone.

♥ **Affirmation:**
I carry light, and I choose to shine with truth, peace, and grace.

INHERITANCE OF FAITH

It's more than stories that bear my name.
It's my faith, a steady flame.
I pass down the gift that cannot fade,
trust in the Divine through night and shade.

Though darkness has fallen many a time
and blinded my eyes,
the sun always graced the skies.

Seeds were planted where the sun would show,
in order for you to see what faith can grow.

Through patient hands, pressed together,
there isn't a trial you can't weather.

Be thankful in all things, come what may,
for each step guides the brighter way.

And as you walk, let your heart ignite.
I pray you carry this forward,
adding your light.

- ♥ **Reflection:** Your faith doesn't have to look like mine. It just has to lead you back to the Divine.
- ♥ **Affirmation:** I carry forward what strengthens me, and I release what doesn't.

WALK FREE

When life will test and shadows fall,
remember, beloveds, you're graced through all.
You are not the world's design,
you are God's beloved, wholly divine.

Walk free, my dear ones, hold your ground.
In faith and love, let truth abound.
Free from fear, from doubt, from shame,
for Heaven itself has called your name.

Let kindness guide each path you tread.
Let peace be where your spirit's led.
When storms arise, when voices sway,
stand firm, let prayer light your way.

You carry the prayers of those before,
their hope, their strength, forevermore.
Each step you take, each seed you sow,
is legacy's bloom, the faith we know.

- ♥ **Reflection:** Walking free is part of the inheritance you deserve to claim.
- ♥ **Affirmation:** I carry forward what strengthens me, and I release what doesn't.

For my grandchildren, Maya Rose and Roman
my living legacy, my joy, and my reminder that love always outlives us.

YOUR SUPERPOWER IS YOU

There's a superpower.
It's in just being you.

When the world feels heavy
and your spirit feels bruised,
remember, my beloveds, what I've always known:
there's greatness in you, planted and grown.

Some will point out flaws.
That's what people do.
But never let their shadows cover your view.

Listen to wisdom, let it refine.
Guard your light; it was made divine.

Every part of you, the strong,
the unsure, the broken, the bright,
all of it is pure.

Lean into your being, let it unfold.
For every piece tells a story untold.

Use what you've learned to lift someone's pain,
to water dry hearts like healing rain.

But don't give away so much of your fire
that you lose your soul in someone else's desire.

You are needed.
There's a superpower within you.

I am your Nana, and this truth is true:
your superpower is simply being you.

Don't let the world squeeze your colors to gray.
Shine as you are, come what may.

You hold gifts no one else can find,
treasures of heart and brilliance of mind.

If they don't love you right, let them go.
You'll still rise, you'll still glow.

And when sorrow comes, as it sometimes will,
pray through the storm. Be quiet. Be still.

The night will pass, as all nights do,
and dawn will remind you God is in you too.

Your light is your strength.
Your softness is your power.
Your voice is your freedom.
Your love is your finest flower.

Let the world see your shine, not because you are flawless,
but because you are whole, courageous, and honest.

Every scar will tell of the battles you've won.
Every tear will water the faith yet to come.

Stand tall, my grand beloveds, in all that you do.
You weren't made to blend in but to stand out true.

With grace, with purpose, with heaven's hue,
your superpower will always be
you.

- **Reflection:** Your legacy begins with how you see yourself. Your light teaches others how to find theirs.
- **Affirmation:** My true power is being who God made me to be.

If this book resonated with you, please consider:

- Sharing it with a friend who may need encouragement

- Reaching out via email at isntshegrayt@gmail.com

- Connecting with me on Instagram @isnt_she_grayt, YouTube @isntshegrayt

Your support, reflections, and shared conversations mean more than you know.

ABOUT THE AUTHOR

Tiffany A. Selden is an author, poet, songwriter, and mixed media artist whose work is rooted in faith, healing, and honest expression. Her writing grows from lived experience and is shaped by prayer, reflection, and a deep belief in the restorative power of words.

She is the author of *The Parental Shift: To Whom Much Is Given, Much Is Woven, WORD! A Year of Growth and Intention*, and *A 30 Day Self Care Journal and Positive Affirmation Puzzle Book. Healing Through Expression* was created as a sacred space where pain could be acknowledged, grace received, and healing gently unfold.

Writing and releasing music under the artist name Isn't She Grayt, Tiffany is also the writer of the anthem **All the Things I Ever Wanted to Do*, available on major music streaming services, along with its companion book. Together, they reflect the freedom found in choosing healing, purpose, and self-honoring later in life and echo the same truth carried throughout these pages that it is never too late to become whole or to live in alignment with what God placed within you.

Through her writing, music, and art, Tiffany hopes to encourage others to pause, reflect, and trust that healing is possible one honest word, one quiet prayer, and one brave step at a time.